LEARNING HOW TO PLAY THE HARMONICA BLUES-STYLE

TERRELL M. BEATTY

LEARNING HOW TO PLAY THE HARMONICA BLUES-STYLE

THE #1 SECRET TO PLAYING

THE BLUES IN JUST MINUTES

TATE PUBLISHING
AND ENTERPRISES, LLC

Learning How to Play the Harmonica Blues-Style
Copyright © 2012 by Terrell M. Beatty. All rights reserved.

No part of this publication may be reproduced, stored in a retrieval system or transmitted in any way by any means, electronic, mechanical, photocopy, recording or otherwise without the prior permission of the author except as provided by USA copyright law.

This book is designed to provide accurate and authoritative information with regard to the subject matter covered. This information is given with the understanding that neither the author nor Tate Publishing, LLC is engaged in rendering legal, professional advice. Since the details of your situation are fact dependent, you should additionally seek the services of a competent professional.

The opinions expressed by the author are not necessarily those of Tate Publishing, LLC.

Published by Tate Publishing & Enterprises, LLC
127 E. Trade Center Terrace | Mustang, Oklahoma 73064 USA
1.888.361.9473 | www.tatepublishing.com

Tate Publishing is committed to excellence in the publishing industry. The company reflects the philosophy established by the founders, based on Psalm 68:11,
"The Lord gave the word and great was the company of those who published it."

Book design copyright © 2012 by Tate Publishing, LLC. All rights reserved.
Cover design by Kenna Davis
Interior design by Sarah Kirchen

Published in the United States of America

ISBN: 978-1-61862-341-6
Music / Instruction & Study / General
12.03.14

ACKNOWLEDGMENTS

I give all the praise and glory of this book to God and Him alone.

I want to give thanks to God for allowing me to be born with a musically talented family. My late mother, Agnes Worley Beatty, my late brother, Terry Beatty, and my ever so close twin brother, Jerrell Beatty. My two boys, Trampis, who is turning into an awesome picker, and Cody, who uses his voice and talents to sing and share the Gospel with confused and troubled youth.

Now, being born into so much musical talent would seem to be all you could want, but when God does something, He does it right, and it is usually more than you would expect. So after I asked God in prayer to send me the wife he wanted me to have, He did. God not only sent me a musically talented lady, He sent me the backbone of my whole ministry, and she is the best help-mate I could have ever dreamed of or imagined. She is Letty Mocha Beatty.

Letty, I thank you so much for all of your God sought help. Most of all I thank God for sending you to me so we can work together to build up the Kingdom of God!

TABLE OF CONTENTS

Foreword 9

Introduction 13

SECTION 1:
HARMONICA NECESSITIES

Choosing the Right or Best Harmonica 19

Knowing Your Harmonica 21

The First Thing You Need to Know About
Playing the Harmonica Blues-Style (The Secret) 25

Key Conversion Chart 27

Taking Care of Your Harmonica 29

SECTION 2:
HOW TO PLAY THE HARMONICA BLUES-STYLE

How to Properly Cup and Hold
the Harmonica (Volume Control) 33

Learning to Play One Hole at a Time 35

Learning to Play Two or Three Holes at a Time 37

Playing a Rhythm on the Harmonica:
Practice, Practice, Practice 39

One Complete Rhythm Circuit Chart. 41

Learning to Slur and Slide your Rhythm. 43

Choking or Bending the Notes on the Harmonica. 45

Double-Choking or Double-Bending
the Holes on the Harmonica. 49

Learning to Find the Right High Note and Working
Down to a Lower Note (Hole Number Four) 51

Learning an All-Hole Sequence Slide, Choke, or
Bend on the Harmonica 53

Learning to Trillo the Harmonica. 57

The Vibrator Bar or Vibrator on the Harmonica 59

SECTION 3:
SOUND EFFECTS

Acoustics 63

Playing the Harmonica Using a Microphone. 65

SECTION 4:
PRACTICE

The Importance of Practice 69

How Should I practice, and What Should I Practice First? . . . 71

FOREWORD

"Honey, I am going to write a book."

"Really," I said, "About what?"

"*How to Play The Harmonica Blues Style.*"

Well if there is one thing I know about my husband, he can definitely play a harmonica. Write a book? …Not so much.

Terrell and I first met in a grocery store, yes a grocery store. Not in the produce section, but in their small cafe. We had both taken lunch from our respective jobs, to have a quick bite at the deli cafe. You know how when you eat and someone is across from you, it seems like every time you look up you catch the others eye. Yep, we would smile, nod our head then quickly look down. As I was leaving, I knew never to pass up an opportunity in direct sales, so I gave him one of my cards. He in turn gave me his. In the corner of his "Furniture Refinishing" card were the words *JESUS FIRST*. I smiled and said I liked that. He said, "You know why I did that?" Many answers came to my mind, but I just shook my head, no. "Because," he said, "I know that with Christ I can do anything, and without him, nothing matters."

Well that was the beginning of a wonderful journey. I had made some choices in my life, and even though I knew

Christ as my Savior, I admit I didn't always consult with Him. At this time in my life I had finally realized He knew what was best for me, so I asked the Lord to put me with the one He had chosen. I was meeting him in the cafe at the local grocery store!

Of the many things we discovered we had in common, music was one of the greatest. I had been so blessed to be able to sing, and although I had had the opportunity to sing all genres of music, I always felt my voice and spirit soar when I was singing of my Savior.

Terrell, I soon found out, had had the same experience. Although Terrell has a wonderful voice, his real talent lay in picking up instruments of all kinds and making music. The best by far...the harmonica.

Terrell once said, "You know, Letty, the hardest and the easiest instrument for me was the harmonica. I have always been fascinated with the little ten hole thing, but no matter how much I tried or how much I read, I couldn't make it sing." He continued, "Then one day I was talking to the Lord, I told him of how much I noticed people like the harmonica, and how it would make them smile, and I sure would like to play it. From that moment, I put myself in an empty room, and after a whole day of working on it, it began to sing! The Lord gave me the harmonica, and I use it praise and honor Him with all styles of music."

Now Terrell wants to share with you. Share the praise yes, but also share what he could never find, in all the books he read, trying to understand the harmonica.

So…he's going to write a book. I would see him walking around with a pad and pen, no computer for him, taking time each night to write. Then one day I sat down and took a deep breath and began to read. I know this sounds bad, but I was amazed! The style, the depth, so complete, yet so simple. I looked up as he came into the room and saw me reading. "Terrell," I said with awe and love in my voice, "This is inspired, oh my goodness!"

He smiled. A smile I know well. A smile that carried me back to the first time we met in the grocery store cafe, when he said, "You know why? Because with Christ I can do anything, without Him nothing matters."

May you be inspired.

—Letty Mocha Beatty

INTRODUCTION

Nearly everybody has or has had that little ten-hole instrument called a harmonica at some point in their lives. Nearly everybody dearly loves to hear someone play the harmonica in a song. Most people, including myself thirty years ago, are just totally fascinated with how a harmonica player gets all the sounds out of a harmonica that looks identical and only has ten holes, and it seems to be just like mine. Well even if you have the same identical kind of harmonica that you have heard professional musicians play, it won't actually make your playing sound like the professional. Well, why is that? I could blow air on the harmonica, but there was just something that I could not figure out. How was the professional using the same harmonica I had and making a choking or bending sound? The sound that a train whistle would make and the rhythm of the starting of the train's wheels as it began to move down the track. I thought that if our harmonicas, the professional's and my own, were the same, there had to be something he had that I didn't.

My wife and I were moving out of an apartment we had been renting and into a house we had bought. As I was making my last trip back to the apartment where I was to meet my landlord to finish up my business of moving out, I found myself with some time to kill waiting on my landlord to show up. So I had always had a harmonica in my truck console, and I would from time to time play around with it. I took the harmonica back inside that empty apartment with me because I knew of a few songs on the guitar and how great it was to play in an empty room, where the acoustics were great.

Well, needless to say, that empty apartment and its acoustics made the harmonica really sound great. I played the guitar, banjo, and keyboard and knew that acoustics were important, and the effects of that empty apartment were giving me a reverb sound that's in PA systems and amps today. Having the great acoustics made my practicing on the harmonica much more enjoyable.

That day and that day alone, in that empty apartment with great acoustics, was where I started to hear and learn how to choke and bend a note on the harmonica and how to play a rhythm. I was totally excited. I had found their *secret* that day; the secret to playing the harmonica and to hearing what seemed to be the same sounds that I had heard the professional harmonica players play.

That day I played the harmonica all day long, even after I had left that empty apartment. Well, what a difference a day makes, and I was wondering if I was going to be able to play the same sound that next day. Well the next day came, and when I woke up that morning, I started playing what I had been playing the day before. It was then that maybe I had figured out that I was onto something, and I had discovered some of the sounds that professional harmonica players make on that little ten-holed instrument.

Having been able to figure out some of these sounds on the harmonica caused me to play and practice each day. What I learned that day really comes down to just about two things: choking and bending a note (a single note, that is) and playing a rhythm.

I believe that it is of the utmost importance when you are practicing to find the room in your house with the best acoustics. Most houses will have at least one or maybe two rooms that have fair acoustics. The acoustics will help you *feel* and *hear* each sound that you are trying to accomplish.

Even when you begin to choke or bend and play a rhythm, you're still only at the beginning of what takes practice and commitment. So just go for it, have fun, enjoy yourself, and thank God that he has given you a desire to want to play.

SECTION 1: HARMONICA NECESSITIES

First and foremost:

> Rejoice in the Lord always, I will say it again: Rejoice! Let your gentleness be evident to all. The Lord is near. Do not be anxious about anything, but in everything, by prayer and petition, with thanksgiving, present your requests to God. And the peace of God which transcends all understanding, will guard your hearts and your minds in Christ Jesus.
>
> Philippians 4:4-9 (NIV)

> I can do all things through Christ which strengtheneth me.
>
> Philippians 4:13 (KJV)

> Delight yourself in the Lord and he will give you the desires of your heart.
>
> Psalm 37:4 (NIV)

> Sing praises to God, sing praises
> Sing praises to our King, sing praises.
> For God is the King of all the earth;
> Sing to him a Psalm of praise.
>
> Psalm 47:6, 7 (NIV)

CHOOSING THE RIGHT OR BEST HARMONICA

Choosing the right and best harmonica is very important. I think that there are a lot of things to take into consideration when choosing a harmonica, but the most important are:

1. CHOOSE A HARMONICA THAT HAS A HARD PLASTIC REED HOLDER.

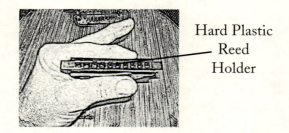

Hard Plastic Reed Holder

There are three types of reed holders that I know of which are made of wood, plastic, and ceramic. I definitely do not recommend a wood reed holder. Wood will swell and cause the reed to come in contact with the edge of the reed holder. Wood reed holders will make your mouth and lips very sore after playing awhile. I have tried ceramic reed holders only once or twice. They seemed to be okay but usually have a huge price when buying them. I use plastic reed holders because they don't swell and don't make your mouth or lips sore, and they are moderately priced. The quality of the plastic reed holder is great and the harmonica, when kept up properly, will last a long time.

2. CHOOSING THE RIGHT AND BEST HARMONICA.

Choose a harmonica that has a good quality sound. Most music stores have a tester. Make sure you have the salesperson run your harmonica through each hole. Make sure the salesperson blows air in and out of each hole. Make sure that each hole has a good, clean sound and you don't hear a rattling of the reed coming in contact with the reed holder. Stores will not let you personally try a harmonica for yourself. So listen real carefully at each hole. When you purchase a harmonica, try it out and make sure it is okay. They will probably take it back if it's not, but don't wait a long period of time to take it back.

I am personally partial to M. Horner's "Special 20" or M. Horner's "Golden Melody." They both have great quality and sound.

KNOWING YOUR HARMONICA

A harmonica has many parts and features. For your information, I will tell you about each part and their function. The harmonica just to look at looks simple, as simple as having ten holes and you blow and suck air in and out of it. That small instrument has a lot more on the inside than what you can imagine by only looking outwardly at it.

Now for what you need to know about playing the harmonica blues-style is only this: It has ten holes, and the holes are numbered one through ten. They have a stamped key, as in A-G, that tells you what key you are playing in. And the harmonica has a right side and a left side.

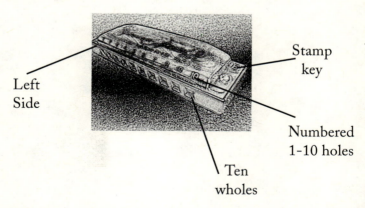

Left Side

Stamp key

Numbered 1-10 holes

Ten wholes

Now the rest of the parts which may interest you go like this:

1. Top and bottom cover
2. Two screw holes that hold covers on
3. Plastic reed holder
4. Ten upper chamber reeds (brass holder)
5. Ten lower chamber reeds (brass holder)

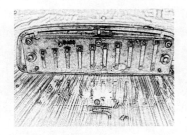

whole divider for entrance and exit air.

Now there are two brass reed holders (upper and lower); they are held together and are separated by what I refer to as the hard plastic reed holder, which is the part that you see and blow air through. Now looking down into each square hole, there is a plastic divider that is for entrance and exit air.

Having this entrance and exit air chambers going to the upper brass reed holder and lower brass reed holder is what keeps you playing without losing breath to play. I guess you could say it is like breathing while you are playing. Suck in and blow out.

Caution: Don't ever take your harmonica apart unless it is totally necessary. The inside is very fine-tuned as to the setting of all twenty reeds to its holder, and taking it apart could damage these parts.

THE FIRST THING YOU NEED TO KNOW ABOUT PLAYING THE HARMONICA BLUES-STYLE (THE SECRET)

The first thing you need to know when you start playing blues-style on the harmonica is: you will play a harmonica marked a different key than the key of the song or the key the instruments are playing in. Well that sounds kind of crazy, doesn't it? But it's definitely not. You would seem to think that if someone is playing the piano or any other instrument in the key of C, you would need a key of C harmonica. Well, that statement is true in one respect. But if you want to play that harmonica blues-style, that first thing you need to realize is that you will be sucking air in the harmonica. Yes, I said suck air in. That's the number-one secret to playing real blues harmonica.

If I blow air outwardly through a C harmonica, that does produce the key of C sound. But when you suck air through the C harmonica, that produces the key of F sound. Just remember the first thing you do playing blues-style is to suck air in on the harmonica. I have written a key conversion chart in the next section that you can use until you memorize the key conversions.

KEY CONVERSION CHART

People who know music and a lot about the different keys such as A, A#, B, Bb, C, D, D#, E, E#, F, F#, and G probably don't have any problem with the different key changes. (E# and F are the same as well as Bb and A#.) For myself, I'm not a music teacher, and I can't even read music. But as we always say down South, "We will play it by ear."

So if you are not familiar with key conversion like myself, you may find the chart below very useful, especially if you need to make a quick key change in a song. It's best if you will memorize the chart below.

KEY CONVERSION CHART

KEY OF MUSIC	STAMPED KEY OF HARMONICA YOU NEED
A	D
Ab	Db
B	E
Bb	Eb
C	F
D	G
Db	F#
E	A
Eb	Ab
F	Bb
F#	B
G	C

TAKING CARE OF YOUR HARMONICA

The inside of the harmonica is very delicate. You can damage the reeds without even knowing it. I also don't recommend using forced air to clean out moisture.

Over my thirty-some years of playing, I have come across people who play the harmonica, and they will literally put the harmonica in a glass of water to give it more of a blues sound. Don't ever do that, because the harmonica will retain too much water. I could not even hear what they were trying to achieve, anyway.

The bottom line is: It does not matter what you do to get the moisture out. It still is just going to have it. Even so, the life of the harmonica will come to an end; then just go buy and replace it.

Taking care of your harmonica is very important. A harmonica's biggest enemy is moisture that will eventually cause corrosion and rust to the sixteen reeds inside. When you are completely done playing, try to get all the moisture out. Even when the harmonica is not in use, it will still breathe. That means air still goes in and out of the harp in an idle state. Corrosion and rust damage will cause the reeds to stick and will cause it to be out of standard tune. So what I do periodically while playing and when I am totally done playing is I will hit it on my leg two or three times to force as much moisture as possible out of it.

The other thing you can do after hitting it on your leg is to keep your harmonica in a soft, tightly closed felt case. Keeping the harmonica in this case is a must. Each harmonica fits so tightly in its place in the case and does not allow airflow and moisture in.

I don't recommend taking the harmonica apart to clean out moisture.

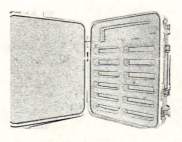

SECTION 2: HOW TO PLAY THE HARMONICA BLUES-STYLE

HOW TO PROPERLY CUP AND HOLD THE HARMONICA (VOLUME CONTROL)

Cupping and holding the harmonica is very important. I consider myself to be a right-handed person. No, you don't have to be just right-handed to play the harmonica. If you are a left-handed person, just do the opposite of what I say and do it opposite of how the diagram shows. The first thing is to always know the right and left sides of a harmonica. Of course, you can pick it up and blow air in and out and find out what side you are on. But on most harmonicas, or at least the ones I play, the right side of a harmonica is the side that has the key letter stamped on it. In certain kinds of light, it is hard to see the small, key-letter stamp.

If you are making music in a band or church group, etc., you don't really want to just start blowing air through it to find out what side you are on. So another thing that you can do is to make or buy some self-adhesive stick-ons. Mark each harmonica with the correct key sticker: an A-sticker for an A-key stamped harmonica, a B-sticker for a B-key stamped harmonica, etc.

Now that you know the right side from the left side of the harmonica, you can learn how to hold it in your hand. Like I said, I am right-handed. So you lefties do the opposite. With my left hand, I pick it up and find the left-hand side of the harmonica. I place the harmonica between my index finger and my thumb on my left hand.

With my right hand, I will bring both hands together to form a cup. The cup of your hand is important because it controls the amount of volume that you want your harmonica to have at certain times in a song. The cup also allows you, the player, to receive some feedback off your hands so you can hear what you are playing.

To increase the volume and to decrease volume, you simply open and close your hands. Open hands for more volume, and close hands for less volume.

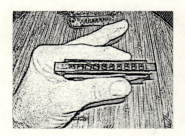 

LEARNING TO PLAY ONE HOLE AT A TIME

I cannot stress enough how important it is to learn to pick out and play only one hole at a time. Just take my word for it how important it is to perform one hole at a time when you play. This will take practice, practice, practice. So start at the first hole and go all the way to the last hole, adjusting your lips to only play one hole. You need to perform this blowing air out and sucking air in at each individual hole. The more you practice, the more you will become familiar with just how much movement it takes when you move from one hole to another hole. There is only a small amount of movement between each hole, and the more you practice moving from one hole to another hole, you will automatically learn to adjust your lips to only fit on one hole at a time. Remember that this step is of the most importance to learn

LEARNING TO PLAY TWO OR THREE HOLES AT A TIME

Playing two or three holes at a time is not as hard as learning to play one hole at a time, simply because of having to not adjust your lips as much to perform the sound you are looking for. Playing two or three holes at a time simply speaks for itself. What I am saying is instead of sucking or blowing air only in and out of one hole, you are sucking and blowing air in and out of two or three holes at a time. The only thing you need to remember about this, is when you blow and suck air in and out of the two or three holes, you must start at the first note (primary note or hole), and include the one or two holes to the right of that primary note.

Example: Fix your lips to suck air in on hole #4 only. Then as you do this, start fixing your lips to include hole #5 and #6.

Practice adding one and two holes to the right of the primary hole. As you master this you will be more than ready for the next section, Playing A Rhythm, as well as the Choking And Bending section ahead.

PLAYING A RHYTHM ON THE HARMONICA: PRACTICE, PRACTICE, PRACTICE

Playing a rhythm on the harmonica consists of simply two sucks of air in and two blows of air out. After each suck or blow of air, you cut the amount of air off with your tongue. Well, you might say, "How do you do this with your tongue?" Do this: Without the harmonica at your mouth, just take two rapid sucks in and two rapid blows out. When you take two rapid sucks in and two rapid blows out, use your tongue to cut off the amount of air coming in and out of the harmonica. To limit the amount of air coming in and out, you will need to allow your tongue to touch the top of your mouth just behind your top teeth. This may seem very awkward, but it is a must that you learn to do it.

Another way to describe this cutting off of air process is this: Have you ever blown a whistle that a referee uses in a basketball game? Most of the time, the referee will make short blows, especially if there is a foul. Now he only blows out on the whistle, but the way he makes the sound short instead of a long-sounding whistle is that he cuts off the amount of air by letting his tongue touch the top of his mouth just behind his top teeth. Try this: Get a referee's whistle, even if you have to buy one, and make the short whistle sound. Blow the whistle very quickly, as if you were calling a foul on a basketball player. While you are blowing the whistle the way I just described, pay close attention as to where your tongue goes when you blow a short, quick blow. This blowing-of-the-whistle tongue action is the same way you limit the amount of in and out air on the harmonica.

Now depending on the tempo or the speed of what you are playing or the song you are playing with, the rapid movement of your tongue to the top of your mouth just behind your top teeth will vary. A fast-tempo song will cause your tongue to limit the amount of air in and out very rapidly. A slow-tempo song will be just the opposite.

The holes on the harmonica are numbered one through ten. Start at hole number two, suck in two times, blow out two times. Then move down to hole number one, suck in two times, blow out two times. Then back to hole number two and repeat. Keep it up, and you build your rhythm.

Note: The rhythm starts at hole number two.

When you are doing this, practice using your tongue like we talked about in the example of a referee's whistle. Then practice the same thing, but try to get faster and faster each time you practice. It's not a matter of seeing how fast you can get. Just remember that songs have a slow, medium, and fast tempo or song speed. Another thing to remember is that wherever you start with two sucks in, don't move down until you have blown two blows out at the same location.

ONE COMPLETE RHYTHM CIRCUIT CHART

This chart will give you the procedure to make one complete rhythm circuit. Once you learn how to play one complete rhythm circuit and perform it slow or fast tempo, you have it. All that rhythm is, is playing one complete rhythm circuit in repetition. The faster you get with performing the rhythm, the more the rhythm sounds as if you are slurring the sound.

There is a section in my book on learning to slur your rhythm. That will come later. For now, it is vital and very important to learn the basic rhythm.

ONE COMPLETE RHYTHM CIRCUIT CHART

First: Take two sucks in at hole # two.

Second: Blow two blows out at hole # two.

Third: Move down to hole #1 and take two sucks in.

Fourth: Blow two blows out at hole # 2

Repeat

Note: Remember to cut off the amount of in and out air with your tongue.

Practice the chart's directions until you get to where you don't have to hardly even think about your ins and outs of air and hole changes.

LEARNING TO SLUR AND SLIDE YOUR RHYTHM

The last section taught you how to do the rhythm on the harmonica. I believe that choking or bending the notes is one of the two most important parts of performing. The second part that is the most of importance is the rhythm. You must get these two parts where you are fairly good, or great even, performing them. Providing you have got the basic rhythm performance where you can easily perform it, you can then start performing what I call "slurring your rhythm."

You know that a rhythm is two sucks and two blows out, and then starting over and over doing the same performance. Now slurring your rhythm is kind of like saying I'm performing the rhythm at a glance. So start performing a rhythm, and work yourself in on doing it faster and faster. The faster you get at performing the actual rhythm will give you the sound effect of a train starting up its wheels, and as it gets to moving, the wheels get faster and faster.

Also, when you have learned this slurring of the rhythm, you can add this part to it. When you have the in-and-out rhythm going as fast as you can, just simply slide your harmonica to the right about three or four holes up from the hole number four as fast as you can, and then slide the harmonica back to the hole number four as fast as you can. This slurring is a great add-on to your total performance.

PART 1: SLURRING CHART

1. Start your rhythm at hole number four and hole number three.

2. Start rhythm off slow and then do the rhythm faster and faster until it becomes a slur.

PART 2: SLURRING CHART

1. Start your rhythm at hole number four and hole number three.

2. Perform the rhythm as fast as you can.

3. Slide your harmonica up three or four holes quickly and back three or four holes quickly from hole number four.

Note: When I say rhythm, I am saying two sucks in and two blows out.

CHOKING OR BENDING THE NOTES ON THE HARMONICA

Most people love to hear a harmonica player make the sound of a train blowing its whistle, and right after that sound, the harmonica player will play the rhythm that we discussed in an earlier section to imitate the wheel revolutions on the train. That sound of a train blowing its whistle is done on the harmonica by what is called "choking" or "bending" a note or several notes. If you are playing a ten-holed harmonica, this "choking" or "bending" can be performed on all ten holes. The secret of "choking" and "bending" notes has to be performed at the right time in a song. Now, that right time can be different in each and every song.

Choking is always performed when you suck air in the harmonica, not when you are blowing air through it. The way or one way you can get familiar or practice choking is to put a piece of Scotch tape over holes one, two, and three, and five, six, and seven, and leave hole four uncovered. For right now, don't worry about holes eight, nine, and ten. After you have covered holes one, two, three, five, six, and seven with Scotch tape, start sucking air through uncovered hole number four and let your tongue go to the bottom of your mouth, with the tip of your tongue just behind your lower teeth. Then do it again and try to limit the amount of air you are sucking through hole number four. When you limit or restrict the air flow you are sucking through hole number four and letting your tongue go to the bottom of your mouth, start visualizing in your mind that you are trying to suck the least amount of air you can through the hole, and at the same time, suck the air in as forcefully as you can. The combination of the least amount of air and letting your tongue drop and the force you use to suck in will determine how much or how little the hole will choke or bend.

Now in order to suck in and drop your tongue to the bottom of your mouth and suck the small amount of air in with force, you are on your way to successfully choking and bending the notes. Don't give up on practicing this because this is very critical in any performance with the harmonica. If it happens to you like it did for me, it may come to you when you least expect it. Try to practice this process in a room with good acoustics, because the acoustics of a room will allow you to hear sounds you may not hear in a room that has acoustics that are not good. Try to remember everything you are attempting to do, because when you least expect it, you may hear what you are listening for. So remembering everything and every way will allow you to repeat the sound you are looking for when it happens.

CHOKING OR BENDING STEPS

1. Cover holes 1, 2, 3, 5, 6, 7 with Scotch tape. Leave hole four uncovered.

2. Start sucking air in on hole number four.

3. Let your tongue go to the bottom of your mouth, with the tip of your tongue just behind your lower teeth.

4. Limit the amount of air you are sucking in by adjusting your lips around hole four.

5. When you are in the process of performing steps one through four, start sucking the air in as forcefully as you can.

Note: When you have learned steps one through five, you can twiddle your tongue to create a sound to add along with the choke. Twiddle your tongue back and forth, up and down, and from side to side. Listen to each sound any time your tongue moves.

DOUBLE-CHOKING OR DOUBLE-BENDING THE HOLES ON THE HARMONICA

You may be saying that I'm still trying to learn how to just choke or bend a hole. So how can I choke a hole, and as I'm choking, take the same hole and choke it beyond the actual choking point? Well in some instances, this can be performed. But what I am going to tell you to do will give you the sense of what it actually sounds like. It does sound like a double-choke or bend.

The first thing you have to do is make sure you can do the section in this book on choking or bending the notes on the harmonica. After you get good at choking a note or a single hole, the second thing you do first is choke hole number four. Then right after you choke hole number four, blow air through hole number four. Then move down to hole number three and choke hole number three, and right after you choke hole number three, blow air through hole number three. By moving down to hole number three, performing a choke and blowing air through hole number three will give you the sound effect of performing a double-choke on just hole number four. Now the second part of performing a double-choke or double-bend is this: Just before you start the steps of a double-choke, move up to hole number five and only suck air in to choke hole number five, and then proceed to perform the first part of the double-choke. The reason for performing this double-choke or bend is it gives you the feeling of a train that has just passed by you, and you hear it going on down the track.

Once you learn the double-choke, it will add a lot to your performance.

DOUBLE-CHOKE CHART

Part One:

1. Choke hole number four, and blow air through hole number four.

2. Move down to hole number three, and choke it and blow air through.

Part Two:

1. Just before you perform part one, go to hole number five and only suck air in to choke hole number five.

2. Then proceed to perform Part One.

Note: Both parts one and two need to be performed quickly in sequence.

Note: You have to already be able to perform the choking or bending of each individual hole before you can double-choke a harmonica.

LEARNING TO FIND THE RIGHT HIGH NOTE AND WORKING DOWN TO A LOWER NOTE (HOLE NUMBER FOUR)

This section is what I call just another part of the performance that is an add-on to the performance. Choking and bending a note and performing the basic rhythm are the main two parts that determine if the right high note can be performed or not. Finding the right high note is usually performed when you get real familiar with playing the harmonica, but it doesn't have to be like that. You may find this section the easiest to learn first, but not usually.

Every harmonica has its own high note. It does not matter which key the harmonica is. So let's find the right note. Starting at hole number four, perform a choke or bend. Hold the choke, and as you are in the actual choke, slide the harmonica quickly—and I mean very, very quickly—to the seventh hole, and choke it quickly and slide the harmonica back to the fourth hole. Like I said earlier, it does not matter what key the harmonica is; the action you take on finding the right high note is the same. As a basic rule, the starting point on a harmonica is at hole number four.

RIGHT HIGH NOTE STEPS

1. Choke or bend hole number four.

2. As you are choking hole number four, move very, very quickly to hole number seven, and perform choke.

3. When you have choked hole number seven, move very, very quickly back to hole number four.

Depending on what song you are playing with, you can sometimes repeat the high-note step more than once.

You can also perform these steps differently if you want to if the song or the rhythm of the song allows you to do so. Instead of sliding back and forth from the fourth note to the seventh note, you can just slide up to the seventh hole and then immediately go back to the fourth hole and do it again over and over, depending on what you are performing.

LEARNING AN ALL-HOLE SEQUENCE SLIDE, CHOKE, OR BEND ON THE HARMONICA

An all-hole sequence slide, choke, or bend is another part of playing the harmonica that is very exciting to perform. After you have really got a good feel of learning to play and choke one hole at a time (that you learned to do in an earlier section), you are now ready to perform a proper choke or bend of each note (that you also learned to do in an earlier section) that will make you ready to perform an all-hole sequence slide, choke, or bend on the harmonica. When you get to where you can perform this all-hole sequence slide choke, it will make your audience say, "How does he do that? He really knows what he is doing with that harmonica." Now when I say or used the word he, I am referring to he or she. I personally know that females are just as good, and in some cases a lot better, than me. But for this book's sake, I will use the word he.

Okay, let's learn to perform an all-hole sequence choke or bend. Go to about the sixth hole, and begin to choke the harmonica. When you are in the deepest sound of the choke with one hand, slide the harmonica as fast as you can to the left. Perform this anywhere from two to three times in a row. After you have performed this two to three times, on your last slide to the right on the harmonica, immediately start performing the in-and-out rhythm that you learned in an earlier section. These two steps go hand-in-hand with each other.

Steps 1 and 2: All-Sequence Slide and Choke (or Bend) Chart

Part 1 (This part shows you how to start at hole number six):

1. Perform a choke or bend on hole number six.

2. In the deepest or lowest part of the choke, slide the harmonica quickly to the *right* to the one and two holes, and perform an in-and-out rhythm.

3. Every time you slide the harmonica either right or left, try to choke holes one through five as much as possible during the slide.

Note: How many times you perform steps one through three is determined by what song you are playing.

Part 2 (This part shows you how to start with a normal in-and-out rhythm.):

1. Start a normal in-and-out rhythm.

2. Quickly slide the harmonica to the *left* to hole number six, and perform a choke.

3. When you are in the deepest sound of choking hole number six, quickly slide the harmonica back to the *right* and start back performing the normal in-and-out rhythm. When you slide the harmonica either right or left, try to choke holes one through five as much as possible.

Note: How many times you perform steps 1-3 is determined by what song you are playing.

LEARNING TO TRILLO THE HARMONICA

Trillo, or trilling, the harmonica is an exciting part of playing. This is just what you might say is an add-on to your performance. Trillo or trilling is the sound you would sometimes hear in a performance that comes mostly at the end of the choke or bending of a note. When you perform a choke, you can make the choke mild or very hard. Choking the harmonica very hard is sometimes referred to as performing what seems like a double-choke. You actually choke the harmonica, and then as this choke is being done, you actually choke the choke sound itself. Double-choke is in another section for you to learn. But whether it is a single- or double-choke, you can perform the trillo or trilling of the harmonica at the very end of the choke.

So the way to perform the trillo sound is to start choking a note. Then at the end of the choke, take the harmonica with the hand that works best for you and begin to very, very rapidly move the harmonica from right to left; only include two holes before or two holes after the hole you are choking.

Try to keep your lips as moist as possible. That will make the harmonica slide from right to left very easily. This performance of trillo or trilling is very exciting to perform and adds a lot to your performance.

THE VIBRATOR BAR OR VIBRATOR ON THE HARMONICA

There is actually no bar on the harmonica that will cause the sound to vibrate. I use the terminology so you would know what I mean, because most people have seen the actual vibrator bar and its effects on a guitar. For the harmonica, the vibrator or vibration effect is done by allowing the hand that is not holding the harmonica to beat in a repetitious way against the hand that is holding the harmonica. That may be a bit awkward to visualize what I am saying. Look at the diagram to see what it looks like or how to perform it. Sometimes you need to perform it according to what song you are playing.

VIBRATOR STEPS

Practice

1. Start choking or bending a note.

2. Start the choke and go through the choke until you are almost all the way complete, and then at the end almost, take the hand that you are not holding the harmonica with and repetitiously beat the hand you are holding the harmonica with. (It is as if you were trying to clap your hand while holding the harmonica.)

SECTION 3: SOUND EFFECTS

ACOUSTICS

Acoustics are exactly what the word sounds like. When you say the word acoustic, it almost or does make you stop and take note of the sounds around you. Does the sound you hear have a flat, dull sound, or does it have a mellow, deep sound, or possibly an echo?

I personally think that acoustics play a big, tremendous part in as to what you would like to hear when you are listening to or playing the harmonica. I think that acoustics come from hearing a train on a railroad at different parts of the day. It has always been a desired sound of most people to hear the train's sound very late at night. The sound of the train could either be of a train approaching you, right up on you, or fading as the train is getting farther away. The wheels of the train are giving you the rhythm you play on the harmonica, and the train's whistle gives you the choking or bending of the holes on the harmonica.

Great acoustics could be around you when practicing and playing the harmonica. Almost everybody's home will have a room in it that will make any musical instrument, and especially the harmonica, sound pleasing to hear. I would suggest that you seek out that room or a place that will give you the feedback of sound that will make practicing and playing enjoyable. It will also make practicing and learning much easier. If it is next to impossible to find the right place to get good acoustics, don't think that is something you can't do without. There are always other options that you can learn in the section on using a microphone with an amplifier or PA system.

PLAYING THE HARMONICA USING A MICROPHONE

Playing through a microphone can be a lot of fun, especially if the sound system you are playing through has great reverb or special effects. While holding the harmonica in one hand, take the microphone in the other hand and join the two together. Now you have to be careful and make the necessary adjustments on the sound equipment to make sure the microphone is not too hot. A hot microphone means that the settings on the sound equipment is too high. The playing of a harmonica through a hot microphone can cause you to be extremely too loud when playing along with other musicians. My suggestion with playing with a microphone is to have good reverb, and set the volume of the microphone on the sound equipment to a lower volume setting. Most settings on sound equipment are numbered one through ten, with ten being the hottest. So I would set the microphone volume between one and five. Now sometimes, depending on what you are performing on the harmonica, you may even have to pull the microphone away from the harmonica to keep the sound from being too loud. Now if you have a great sound person, he can compensate for the loud sound on the mixing board in the sound booth. But most of the time, you will just have to remember to pull the microphone away from the harmonica yourself.

SECTION 4: PRACTICE

THE IMPORTANCE OF PRACTICE

Practice will cause you to become more and more efficient. Our daily lives are really set up on a schedule. Whether you realize it or not, being on the same schedule each day causes you to become very efficient. Although our daily schedules are similar in style, we all look and seek after what is the best and easiest way to make our schedules as efficient as we can. It's not that we are looking for the easy way of becoming efficient, but it's because we tend to choose the style that works best for us. I believe that our individual styles differ from each other. It's almost like fingerprints. We are all different. Whether our daily schedules are something that we love to do or something that we have to do, it all comes down to a repetitious thing we do day in and day out. That repetition will cause us to become very efficient. Now practicing the harmonica and having a desire to become a harmonica player will come down to how bad you want it. Are you going to set aside some time each day to practice?

Practice makes perfect. We all have heard that saying about practice. Why do people say that practice makes perfect? Well, we will never reach total perfection on or at anything until Jesus comes back, but until he does, we can all strive to be as good as we can. How do we come to be the best we can at anything? Practice, practice, practice.

Now take people like Roy Clark, Kenny Rogers, John Lennon, and any other notable performers. Their styles are different in writing music, singing, and playing musical instruments. In the many hours and years that they put into practice, practice, practice, it all comes to their one and only style of performing. When you make up your mind to dedicate and sacrifice your time to practice, practice, practice, it will be then that you start your own style, and who's to say that your own particular style will be developed and you will receive the same recognizable attention as some of the performers we mentioned earlier? Your recognizable attention all depends on how badly you want to learn how to play the harmonica and your dedication and sacrifice of your time. The sky is the limit. So what are you going to do? Go for it. Practice, practice, practice.

HOW SHOULD I PRACTICE, AND WHAT SHOULD I PRACTICE FIRST?

Practice starts when you make up your mind that you realize that in order for yourself to become as good as you can, you must practice. You must even practice to train your mind that you have to sacrifice some time each day because of your need for being the best harmonica player that you can be. I also don't suggest that you allow yourself to become obsessed with learning to play. When we are overly obsessed with anything, we actually are allowing it to rule over us or become a so-called god of our lives. I know that you probably know people who allow things like golf, baseball, basketball, and others that will totally dominate their lives. I believe that everything should be done in moderation. Even when you decide to start practicing the harmonica, do it in moderation. Overdoing anything causes conflict in your personal relationships with God, family, and friends. It can also cause you to become disinterested totally. So just make up your mind to start practicing, and practice moderately every day or maybe just every other day. I personally think that practicing every other day will decrease the possibility of burnout, and it will give your brain time to get refreshed. You need to realize that learning to play the harmonica blues-style is a totally new process for your brain. Now don't get me wrong. I will have to admit that when I have an interest in doing or accomplishing something, I will go at it whole hog. I am a very competitive person and I am a good loser, but I don't like to lose. I guess the best way to say it is this: Don't do as I just said I have done sometimes, just do what I am trying to say.

Now you may be thinking, *what should I start practicing first?* I think you should memorize the Key Conversion Chart. This key conversion chart does not have anything to do with physically playing the harmonica. The chart only lets you know what key of harmonica you need when you know what key the music you are playing with is in. Remember that I told you that the first thing you need to do when playing blues-style harmonica is to suck air in the harmonica, not blow air out. Example: blowing air out of a harmonica that is stamped the key of C is the key of C. Now when sucking air in on a harmonica stamped key of C, you will hear the sound or key of F.

The next thing I would practice would be getting used to properly holding and cupping the harmonica. Hold the harmonica in your dominant hand. My dominant hand is my left. Then take your other hand and learn to cup it around your dominant hand. Learning to use your cupping hand is important because it allows you to adjust the correct amount of volume you need at different points of the music.

After you have gotten used to holding the harmonica, you are now ready for learning to play the rhythm. What I am about to tell you now is what I consider the two most important practicing parts. It is a must that you learn to play rhythm and learn to choke or bend the holes. I'm not going to tell you that this is a set way to practice these. Just remember that they are actually the backbone in playing the harmonica blues-style. When you learn to do these two parts of playing the harmonica, the other parts will come easily.

PRACTICE GUIDE

1. Have a mental commitment to practice and sacrifice time each day or every other day.

2. Practice in moderation. Don't overdo it and get burned out quickly.

3. Memorize the Key Conversion Chart.

4. Practice sucking air in on just one hole. Learn how to adjust your mouth on one hole.

5. Practice proper holding of the harmonica in the right hand and properly cupping with the left hand.

TWO MOST IMPORTANT PRACTICING STEPS

1. Learn how to perform rhythm. Use the Rhythm Circuit Chart.

2. Learn how to choke or bend each hole. Use the "Choking or Bending the Notes" section.